American Leaders & Innovators
Colonial Times to Reconstruction

Author: Victor Hicken, Ph.D.
Consultants: Schyrlet Cameron and Suzanne Myers
Editor: Mary Dieterich
Proofreaders: April Albert and Margaret Brown

COPYRIGHT © 2019 Mark Twain Media, Inc.

ISBN 978-1-62223-768-5

Printing No. CD-405034

Mark Twain Media, Inc., Publishers
Distributed by Carson-Dellosa Publishing LLC

The purchase of this book entitles the buyer to reproduce the student pages for classroom use only. Other permissions may be obtained by writing Mark Twain Media, Inc., Publishers.

All rights reserved. Printed in the United States of America.

Visit us at www.carsondellosa.com

Table of Contents

Introduction 1

Units

Roger Williams 2

Benjamin Franklin 5

James Otis 8

Benjamin Banneker 11

Francis Marion 14

Thomas Paine 17

Joseph Warren 20

John Jay 23

Tecumseh 26

Dolley Madison 29

Winfield Scott 32

Benjamin Lundy 35

David Glasgow Farragut 38

Dorothea Lynde Dix 41

Justin Smith Morrill 44

Harriet Beecher Stowe 47

Elizabeth Cady Stanton 50

Carl Schurz 53

Blanche Kelso Bruce 56

Answer Keys 59

Introduction

> There is little that is more important for an American citizen to know than the history and traditions of his country. Without such knowledge, he stands uncertain and defenseless before the world, knowing neither where he has come from nor where he is going. With such knowledge, he is no longer alone but draws a strength far greater than his own from the cumulative experience of the past and a cumulative vision of the future.
>
> —John F. Kennedy

Students can better understand the world today by learning about the people of yesterday and knowing that they were real people, just like you and me. Through the following biographical sketches, the learner identifies with them as real people. There was never any thought of ranking famous Americans. The principle followed is that there be a happy mix of some of the titanic figures of American History and some of the lesser ones. So it is that here appear the names of Benjamin Franklin, Dorothea Dix, David Farragut, Joseph Warren, and fifteen other biographies. These deal briefly and concisely with people who helped make the republic great.

There are 19 units in *American Leaders & Innovators: Colonial Times to Reconstruction.* Each unit can be used independently or combined with others into a unit of study that covers a specific historical era.

There are three components in each unit:

- The **Reading Selection** helps the student gain depth in factual knowledge.

- The **Recalling Key Details** page checks the student's understanding of the reading selection.

- The **Activity** page offers an enrichment activity to expand the student's knowledge.

The units in this book are designed as stand-alone material for the classroom or homeschool setting. The units can be used as supplemental material to enhance the classroom social studies curriculum, for independent study, or as a tutorial at home.

Roger Williams 1603–1683

READING SELECTION

Roger Williams was born in London to a middle-class family that had obtained some financial success in business. He was educated at Cambridge University. While attending the university, Williams became a Puritan. Puritans were of the Protestant faith and believed in the removal of statues, rituals, and bishops from their form of worship. His time at Cambridge strengthened his views on the relationship between the government and the church and his beliefs concerning religious freedom. Williams' views were directly opposite of the beliefs of the Anglican faith and the Church of England, the national church of England with the English king as the official leader.

Roger Williams statue in Roger Williams Park, Providence, R.I.

After leaving Cambridge, Williams became a minister. His views on religion made him unpopular in England. Not too long after the "Pilgrims" landed at Plymouth in New England, Williams and his family sailed for the New World, arriving in the Massachusetts Bay Colony in 1631. He refused offers to become the minister in one Boston church, but in 1633, he went to Salem to minister to a congregation in that town. Almost immediately, he began to cause trouble with the authorities. Not only did he champion the cause of local Native American tribes, but he began to attack the relationship between the local government and the church. Williams argued for tolerance based upon human dignity and pushed for the separation of church and state. He thought that the government should stay out of the business of the church, and vice versa.

By 1636, Williams was expelled from the colony by the Massachusetts court because of his views on religious freedom and his preaching that the king had no right to grant or charter Native American tribal lands to colonists. Forced to flee, he spent the winter with the Narragansett Native American people. From this tribe, he obtained a land title to what was to be most of Rhode Island. In this area, Williams and his followers set up the settlement of Providence. The colony was more tolerant of other religious beliefs. They separated church beliefs and the governing of the colony.

In 1643, Williams returned to England to seek a charter for the Providence colony. Upon returning to the colonies, Williams continued to serve the Rhode Island settlements, and from 1654 to 1657, he acted as the president of the settlement association.

The tolerance implicit in the Rhode Island charter brought other dissidents to the area. Mrs. Anne Hutchinson, another religious leader, established the settlement of Portsmouth in Rhode Island. The Rhode Island colony became a sanctuary for religious minorities such as Baptists, Quakers, and Jews.

His friendship with the Narragansett people helped maintain peaceful relations between the Native Americans and English settlers until the outbreak of King Philip's War (1675–1676). New England Native Americans, under a leader known as King Philip, arose, burning dozens of towns and killing several hundred settlers. Williams joined with colonial forces as a soldier, even though he was well into his seventies. "King Philip's War" was the last major effort by the Native Americans of the area to drive out the English settlers.

Roger Williams died in Providence, Rhode Island, in 1683. All in all, Williams made two major contributions to American life—the separation of church and state, and religious freedom. These views are thought to have inspired the writers of the U.S. Constitution and the Bill of Rights.

American Leaders & Innovators: Colonial Times to Reconstruction — Roger Williams

Name: _____ Date: _____

Recalling Key Details

1. As a Puritan, what did Roger Williams believe about religious worship?

2. Why did Williams leave England in 1631?

3. What did Williams believe about the connection between church and government?

4. Why was Williams expelled from the Massachusetts Bay Colony?

5. How was Providence colony more tolerant than other colonies?

6. What is the meaning of the word *dissidents* as it is used in paragraph five of the reading selection?

7. What was the greatest contribution of Roger Williams to American government?

American Leaders & Innovators: Colonial Times to Reconstruction   Roger Williams

Name: _____ Date: _____

Activity

In 1643, *A Key Into the Language of America* by Roger Williams was published. In the book, Williams makes observations about the customs and beliefs of the Narragansett people. This is followed by a translation of words and phrases from the Narragansett language to English. The following is an example from his book.

> **Observation**
>
> *In this respect they are remarkably free and courteous, to invite all Strangers in; and if any come to them upon any occasion, they request them to come in, if they come not in of themselves.*
>
> | | |
> |---|---|
> | Awássish | *Warm you.* |
> | Máttapsh yóteg | *Sit by the fire.* |
> | Taûbotneanawáyean | *I thank you.* |
> | Tocketúnnawem | *What say you?* |

Directions: Practice pronouncing numbers in the Narragansett language. Once you have learned all the numbers, take turns with a partner counting to ten in Narragansett.

Number	Narragansett Language	Pronunciation
one	nquit	(n-quite)
two	neesse	(nee-see)
three	nish	(neesh)
four	yoh	(yo)
five	napanna	(na-panna)
six	qutta	(coo-tah)
seven	enada	(ee-nada)
eight	shwosuck	(shwo-suck)
nine	paskugit	(pass-coo-git)
ten	piuck	(pea-yook)

Benjamin Franklin 1706–1790

READING SELECTION

Benjamin Franklin was one of the great men of his age. Along with George Washington, Thomas Jefferson, and Alexander Hamilton, he was among the leading Americans of the Revolutionary and post-Revolutionary periods.

Franklin is often referred to as a "self-made man." He was born into a poor family but became successful through his own efforts. Franklin was born in Boston, the 15th child of 17 children. His father was a candlemaker. Although Franklin attended school for a time, he withdrew and went to work for his father. Continuing to be an avid reader, he read books on algebra, geometry, navigation, grammar, logic, science, French, German, Italian, Spanish, and Latin.

When Franklin was 12 years old, he apprenticed to his brother James, a printer. Aspiring to write, he produced a series of articles under the pen name of "Mrs. Silence Dogood." James, not knowing that Benjamin had written them, printed the articles in his paper. Discovered eventually, Benjamin fled to Philadelphia. Now 17, he worked as a printer and managed to buy his own press in 1730. His newspaper, the *Pennsylvania Gazette,* quickly became a success due to its style and wit.

In 1732, he began the publication of *Poor Richard's Almanack*. The book was printed annually from 1732 to 1758. It included weather and agricultural predictions, charts of the moon's phases, and a series of proverbs such as "Early to bed and early to rise, makes a man healthy, wealthy, and wise."

Meanwhile, his fertile mind and unending energy led him into other projects. He was Philadelphia's postmaster for a while and improved on the mail service. He established special messenger services between certain cities. He started the world's first subscription library. He organized a fire department. He reformed the city police and commenced a program to pave and light the streets of the town. He led the fight to establish a hospital in Philadelphia. Also, he helped to found the American Philosophical Society.

During his scientific endeavors, he studied the relationship of electricity to lightning and conducted his famous kite experiments to prove his point. In between times, he studied the flow of ocean currents and invented a new kind of stove, bifocal glasses, and a rocking chair that could swat flies.

The list of accomplishments in Franklin's life had only begun. He persuaded the British government to repeal the Stamp Act. When the colonies chose the path of independence, he helped write the Declaration of Independence. When the colonies needed military help, he went to France where his charming personality and clever diplomacy helped to persuade the French government to send troops and supplies. He helped to negotiate the preliminary articles of the Treaty of Paris, ending the war between America and Britain. The treaty recognized American independence and sovereignty. He was a representative to the Constitutional Convention, and one of the 39 signers of the Constitution of the United States. His last public act was to sign an appeal to Congress calling for the abolition of slavery in America.

Benjamin Franklin died in April 1790. Approximately 20,000 people attended ceremonies in Philadelphia in his honor. He is the only person who signed all three documents establishing the sovereignty of the United States: the Declaration of Independence, the Treaty of Paris, and the United States Constitution.

American Leaders & Innovators: Colonial Times to Reconstruction — Benjamin Franklin

Name: _____ Date: _____

Recalling Key Details

1. Why is Benjamin Franklin considered a "self-made man"?

2. What is the meaning of the word ***apprenticed*** as it is used in paragraph three of the reading selection?

3. What was the name of the newspaper Franklin published?

4. What type of information was included in *Poor Richard's Almanack*?

5. What projects did Franklin undertake to improve the living conditions in Philadelphia?

6. What was Franklin's major contribution as a diplomat?

7. What was Benjamin Franklin's greatest contribution to the establishment of the United States?

Activity

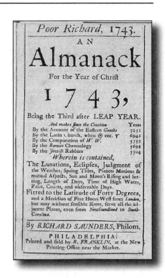

Directions: Read the following proverbs from *Poor Richard's Almanack*. Then write the meaning of each proverb in your own words.

> **Example**
>
> Proverb: Early to bed and early to rise, makes a man healthy, wealthy, and wise.
>
> Meaning: A well-rested person will have the physical and mental energy needed to live a successful life.

1. It takes many good deeds to build a good reputation, and only one bad one to lose it.

2. Whatever is begun in anger ends in shame.

3. Honesty is the best policy.

4. Take time for all things: great haste makes great waste.

5. 'Tis easier to prevent bad habits than to break them.

James Otis 1725–1783

READING SELECTION

James Otis was born in West Barnstable, Massachusetts. Little is known of his childhood, except the probability that he was raised by parents steeped in middle-class traditions. He attended Harvard College and graduated in 1743. He soon began to study law and quickly attained success. In 1756, he was chosen as the king's advocate general of the vice-admiralty court. A few years later, he took on the task of acting as the legal representative of the Boston Merchants in their fight against the British Writs of Assistance.

These Writs gave British officials wide powers in the colonies. Their usage went back to the first half of the eighteenth century, when it was not uncommon for American merchants to be engaged in smuggling goods past royal port collectors. Prior to 1760, the Writs were not widely enforced, however, and smuggling in and out of the colonies had become one of the major enterprises of colonial merchants. When King George III ascended the throne, he requested the renewal of the Writs of Assistance in order to cut American trade to the West Indies. The Writs of Assistance allowed authorized customs officers to enter any premises or area during daylight in order to determine the possibility of illegal importation or smuggling. Otis acted as a counselor to Boston smugglers. He argued in the courts that such writs were "instruments of slavery." Otis lost his case, but he did win public opinion with his arguments.

James Otis was one of the most active of the early Patriots in the American colonies.

From that time on, Otis was quite active in the colonial cause. One of the main grievances of the colonists was taxes imposed by the king and the British Parliament. "Taxation without representation is tyranny" is a famous phrase attributed to Otis. In 1765, Parliament passed the Stamp Act. It required that a revenue stamp be placed on legal documents, newspapers, and marriage licenses. Appeals to Parliament by the colonists to repeal the law had been ignored. James Otis suggested representatives from each colony meet to agree on a united course of action. In 1765, Otis along with other representatives from the colonies gathered together in New York City at the Stamp Act Congress to discuss their complaints. Otis helped create a list of the colonists' grievances that was sent to the King. Due to Otis and other fiery colonial leaders, the Stamp Act was repealed.

Shortly thereafter, however, the British government began to enforce the Townshend Acts upon the colonies. These acts imposed taxes upon various importations to the colonies; they represented an attempt by the British government to insert its authority in a broad way into colonial affairs. Once again, Otis argued against these "illegalities" and urged the Massachusetts colonial government to lead the way in resisting them. When the British asked Massachusetts to "rescind" its actions of revolt, Otis replied, "We are asked to rescind, are we? Let Great Britain rescind her measures, or the colonies are lost to her forever."

James Otis' revolutionary career seemed to be well underway, and with luck he might have assumed a very large role in the events if fate had not intervened. In 1769, Otis was attacked by a group of British revenue officers who resented his criticisms of the British Empire. He suffered a head wound in the attack that had a lasting effect on his mental health. In 1783, the very year of the treaty ending the Revolutionary War, Otis was struck by lightning and killed.

American Leaders & Innovators: Colonial Times to Reconstruction — James Otis

Name: _____ Date: _____

Recalling Key Details

1. What were the British Writs of Assistance?

2. What was Otis' argument against the Writs of Assistance?

3. What is the meaning of the word **grievances** as it is used in paragraph three of the reading selection?

4. What is the meaning of Otis' statement: "Taxation without representation is tyranny."?

5. What was the Stamp Act?

6. What were the Townshend Acts?

7. What were James Otis' major contributions to the colonial cause?

American Leaders & Innovators: Colonial Times to Reconstruction James Otis

Name: _____ Date: _____

Activity

Directions: You are a colonist living in colonial America. You believe it is necessary to write a letter to King George III expressing your grievances concerning the new taxes imposed by the British Parliament. Your letter should contain two paragraphs.
- Paragraph 1: Explain how you feel about his policy of "taxation without representation." Describe how it has affected your life. Give two specific examples.
- Paragraph 2: In your conclusion, suggest solutions to solve the taxation problem.

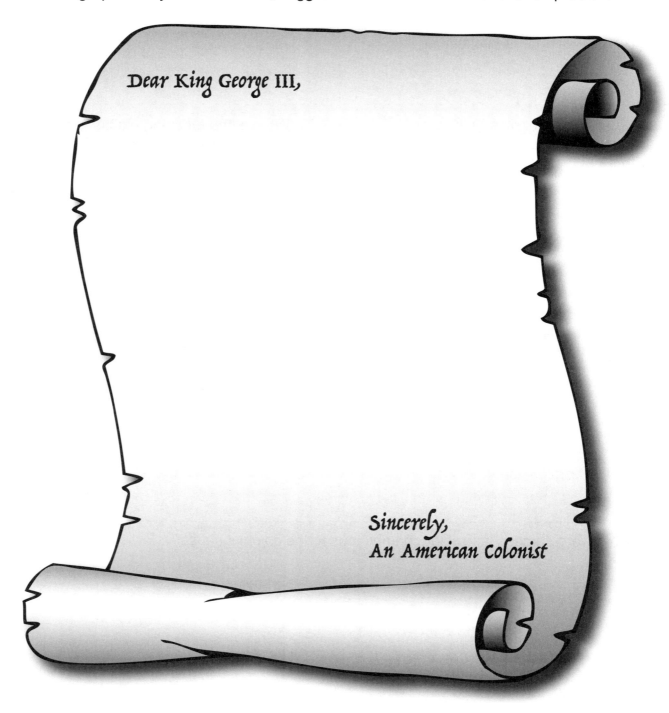

Benjamin Banneker 1731–1806

READING SELECTION

Benjamin Banneker has been called the "most accomplished African American" in the period generally known as the Federalist Era. Banneker was born on his family's farm near Ellicott's Mills, Maryland, on November 9, 1731. As a child, he attended a private Quaker school that educated both African Americans and whites. His father was a former slave and his mother was the daughter of an Englishwoman and a former slave. The family was a "free" family living in a colony in which slavery flourished.

Young Benjamin showed a deep interest in both science and mathematics from the very beginning. He especially enjoyed doing math calculations for his own enjoyment. In 1752, Banneker used his mechanical skills and his knowledge of the workings of a pocket watch to build a wooden clock. The clock is believed to be the first wooden clock built in America. The clock kept correct time for several decades.

This sketch is a likeness of an image of Banneker that appeared on the cover of his almanac.

In 1771, Banneker became acquainted with a white Quaker by the name of George Ellicott, a Maryland flour miller. When the Ellicott mills were under construction, Banneker visited the sites frequently and increased his general knowledge of engineering techniques. Ellicott lent Banneker books on science and astronomy and some astronomical instruments. By 1789, Banneker became so knowledgeable about astronomy and proficient with the instruments that he was able to predict a solar eclipse with a degree of accuracy.

In 1792, Banneker began the publication of a series of almanacs. Information such as weather forecasts and tide tables were included in the almanacs, as well as poems and anti-slavery speeches and essays. The first issue of the almanac contained an account written by one of Banneker's friends as a testimony to the scientist's ability. In it is described a portion of Banneker's early life, how hard he studied when he was young, and how determined he was to succeed.

The almanacs earned for Banneker the respect of men of influence. Secretary of War James McHenry of President Adams' administration not only distributed copies of the almanac but gained important connections for Banneker in society. Banneker even sent a copy of the first almanac to then Secretary of State Thomas Jefferson, who sent it on to the Secretary of the Academy of Sciences in Paris.

As a result of his labors, Banneker was asked to join a survey team led by Major Andrew Ellicott. The team's mission was to set the boundaries of the District of Columbia and to design a layout for the capitol, home of the president, streets, parks, and important public buildings for Washington, D.C., the nation's capital. Pierre L'Enfant was commissioned to be the major plan designer. Later, when L'Enfant resigned, taking the plans with him, Major Ellicott and Banneker worked together to redraw the plans from memory.

Banneker continued to publish his almanacs until 1797. A mathematician, astronomer, scientist, inventor, author, farmer, and surveyor, Benjamin Banneker made major contributions in the area of anti-slavery. He fought the "institution" of slavery, as it was called, until his death in 1806.

American Leaders & Innovators: Colonial Times to Reconstruction   Benjamin Banneker

Name: _____ Date: _____

Recalling Key Details

1. What is noteworthy about the wooden clock built by Benjamin Banneker?

2. How did George Ellicott help to further Banneker's education?

3. What type of information did Banneker include in his almanacs?

4. How did Secretary of War McHenry help to promote Banneker's reputation?

5. To whom did Jefferson send a copy of Banneker's almanac?

6. What is the meaning of the word *survey* as it is used in paragraph six of the reading selection?

7. What contributions did Benjamin Banneker make to the layout and design of Washington, D.C.?

American Leaders & Innovators: Colonial Times to Reconstruction — Benjamin Banneker

Name: _____ Date: _____

Activity

Banneker's Wooden Clock

Directions: Complete the following Internet Scavenger Hunt to learn more about Benjamin Banneker. Use keywords to help you locate the best possible search results.

1. What is the title of Banneker's 1792 almanac?

   Answer:

2. In what year was Banneker featured on a commemorative stamp?

   Answer:

3. What was the main crop grown on Banneker's farm?

   Answer:

4. How was Banneker's wooden clock destroyed?

   Answer:

5. What did Banneker discover about the locust cycle?

   Answer:

Francis Marion 1732–1795

READING SELECTION

Francis Marion was America's best-known guerrilla fighter during the American Revolution. There were other South Carolina militia leaders—Thomas Sumter, Andrew Picken, and Elijah Clarke—but Marion was the most famous. Marion earned the nickname the "Swamp Fox" because of his ability to escape his pursuers in the swamps.

Marion was born on a plantation in South Carolina in 1732. At the age of 15, he signed on as a crewman on a ship headed for the West Indies. The ship sank when it was struck by a whale. He spent several days in a lifeboat without food and water before reaching shore. After the experience, Marion decided not to pursue a naval career.

Marion was not a young man when the American Revolution started. He had been a member of the South Carolina Provincial Congress in 1775, and during the rising unrest against the British, he had voted for war. Joining a group of volunteer fighters, he quickly became a captain. During the fight for Charleston, he sprained his ankle and was forced to leave the battlefield early. This was a stroke of good fortune for him, because so many other American officers were captured. He was left as one of the few free American officers to combat the British in South Carolina.

Francis Marion and his men used guerilla warfare tactics against the British.

Commanding the American forces in the northern part of South Carolina, Marion was forced to improvise. His men were too few in number to give open battle to the British. Neither were they well enough equipped to face even the smaller British detachments. Marion developed a series of strategies that involved surprise attacks and quick withdrawals. He was one of the first to employ these types of tactics against the British. These tactics would become known as "guerrilla warfare."

Since Marion's men had to move about the countryside so rapidly, they were instructed to provision themselves. They did away with cumbersome supply wagons. Marion's blacksmiths made swords from saw blades and farm implements. Pewter plates were melted in order to provide lead for bullets. Ammunition was in such short supply that each man was allowed only three rounds per battle.

Marion's hideout was on Snow Island located in the Pee Dee River. The British searched throughout South Carolina but never came across the guerrilla camp. From Snow Island, Marion made quick raids inside British lines, picking off supplies at one place and driving off horses at another. Occasionally, Marion hit British camps in which American prisoners were being held. In doing this, he was able to free many captured rebels.

Banastre Tarleton, a British cavalry officer, spent much of his time riding about the countryside in search of the Swamp Fox. Tarleton was a professional soldier; Marion's only previous action had been in a small war against Native Americans in the South. Yet, Marion constantly frustrated and eluded Tarleton and his soldiers.

After the war, Marion went back to his Pond Bluff Plantation in South Carolina. The end of the Revolution brought an end to Marion's contributions to the national scene; however, he did go on to serve several terms in the South Carolina legislature. Marion's bravery and style of fighting during the Revolution turned him into a legend in his own time. His legendary fame as an American hero continues even today on television and in movies.

American Leaders & Innovators: Colonial Times to Reconstruction   Francis Marion

Name: _____ Date: _____

Recalling Key Details

1. How did Francis Marion earn the nickname "Swamp Fox"?

2. What life experience persuaded Marion <u>not</u> to pursue a naval career?

3. What happened as a result of Marion's injury during the fight for Charleston?

4. What does the term **guerrilla warfare** mean as it is used in paragraph four of the reading selection?

5. Why was Marion's guerrilla camp never located by the British?

6. Why did British officer Tarleton spend most of his time hunting for the Swamp Fox?

7. What was Francis Marion's major contribution to the American Revolution?

American Leaders & Innovators: Colonial Times to Reconstruction   Francis Marion

Name: _____ Date: _____

Activity

Directions: Francis Marion was a militia leader during the American Revolution. Select one of the other militia leaders mentioned in paragraph one of the reading selection. Research his contribution to the American Revolution. Create a stand-up paper cube to display the information. Add computer-generated graphics or create sketches to add interest to your text.

Stand-up Paper Cube

Step 1: Hamburger fold two sheets of construction paper. Make one side one-half inch longer than the other.

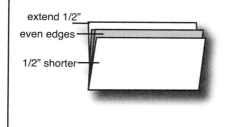

Step 2: On the longer side of each sheet, create a one-half-inch fold. This makes flaps.

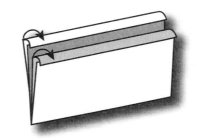

Step 3: On one sheet, place glue along the small folded flap.

Step 4: Place the non-folded edge of the second sheet into the crease and fold the glue-covered flap over this sheet of paper. Repeat steps 3 and 4 with the other flap to create the cube.

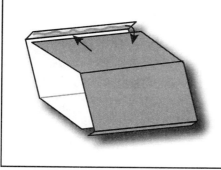

Step 5: The cube can be collapsed flat to place information and illustrations on all sides.

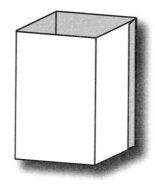

Step 6: Display your cube.

Swamp Fox

Thomas Paine 1737–1809

READING SELECTION

Thomas Paine was never really an American, and his contributions to American history were concentrated in but a few years of activity. Yet, he is remembered today as one of the heroes of the American Revolution.

Paine was born in England. His family was very poor. His formal education at a charity school ended when he was 13 years old. He became an apprentice to his father as a stay-maker. This either meant that he learned to make strong ropes for the masts of sailing vessels or that he made stays, a type of lady's corset. Historians are unclear as to which skill he was learning, since both professions could be called stay-makers. In 1757, he opened his own stay-making shop, but the business collapsed two years later. In 1765, he was fired from his job as a customs officer.

By 1774, Paine was in debt and needed a change. It was at this stage of his life that he met Benjamin Franklin, who suggested he move to the American colonies. Paine came to America and almost immediately became involved in the colonial propaganda activities that preceded the Revolutionary War. In 1776, after the battle at Lexington and Concord, Paine produced the most brilliant statement of American aims in his pamphlet *Common Sense*. What Paine said, essentially, is that America had now come too far to return to the British Empire under the old arrangements. His pamphlet encouraged the colonists to rebel against the British government.

Paine followed this publication with a barrage of other pamphlets and leaflets—the most noted being *The American Crisis*, a series of 16 pamphlets that were meant to inspire the soldiers and patriots to continue to fight after a series of losses to the British. In these are the famous lines: "These are the times that try men's souls. The summer soldier and the sunshine patriot will, in this crisis, shrink from the service of their country..." Almost as much as anything else, Paine's writings held Washington's army together. General Washington read Paine's writings to his troops to boost their morale during the long winter at Valley Forge.

Paine himself served only briefly as a soldier. He continued to occupy minor positions in the newly formed states, and even though he was given rather substantial gifts by Pennsylvania and New York, he was never able to manage his financial affairs properly.

Paine left for France and later England in 1787. In England, he published a defense of the French Revolution in his book *Rights of Man*. Welcomed by the French, Paine worked for the success of the revolution in that country. Once again, however, he managed to antagonize almost everybody and was eventually thrown in jail. While behind bars, he wrote the book *Age of Reason*.

Eventually, President Jefferson arranged for Paine's return to the United States. By this time, Paine was not popular with Americans. They were tired of his continuous harping upon the revolution and were upset with his attack upon the character of George Washington. It seems that Paine had been offended when Washington failed to act to free him from French jails during his imprisonment. Paine died in 1809 and was buried in New York. Ten years following burial, his body was disinterred and removed to England.

While Paine's personal life was filled with turmoil and financial failure, his writings were powerful, and without them, the Revolution may well have failed. *Common Sense* promoted the idea of independence from Great Britain. *The American Crisis* inspired Washington's army to continue fighting at a time when affairs were going badly for the Revolutionary cause.

American Leaders & Innovators: Colonial Times to Reconstruction — Thomas Paine

Name: _____ Date: _____

Recalling Key Details

1. How could Thomas Paine's early life be described?

2. Why did Paine write the pamphlet *Common Sense*?

3. Why did Paine write *The American Crisis* pamphlet series?

4. What is the meaning of the word **patriot** as it is used in paragraph four of the reading selection?

5. Why did General Washington read Paine's writings to his troops?

6. Why was Paine unpopular with Americans after he returned from France?

7. What was Thomas Paine's greatest contribution to American independence?

American Leaders & Innovators: Colonial Times to Reconstruction   Thomas Paine

Name: _____ Date: _____

Activity

Directions: Thomas Paine encouraged American colonists to gain their independence from Great Britain. Read the three famous quotes by Thomas Paine. What do you think Paine was saying to the colonists about their struggle for independence?

1. **Quote:**
"The cause of America is in a great measure the cause of all mankind."

1. **Meaning:**

2. **Quote:**
"It is not in number, but in unity, that our great strength lies; …"

2. **Meaning:**

3. **Quote:**
"Lead, follow, or get out of the way."

3. **Meaning:**

Joseph Warren 1741–1775

READING SELECTION

Joseph Warren was born in Roxbury, Massachusetts, on June 11, 1741. At the age of 14, he enrolled at Harvard College in Cambridge, Massachusetts. Warren was interested in the study of medicine. After graduating from the college in 1759, he continued to learn his profession by performing a kind of apprenticeship with a leading Boston physician. While still in his early twenties, Warren became one of the most respected physicians in the entire Boston area. His patient list included many rebels such as Samuel Adams, John Hancock, Paul Revere, and John Adams.

After the enactment of the Stamp Act of 1765 by the British Parliament, Warren turned to revolutionary activities with great intensity. In 1767, he became the leading spokesman in Boston against the Townshend Acts, which were restrictive British laws being laid upon the colonies. He wrote a series of articles published in the *Boston Gazette* in opposition to the acts and signed them "a True Patriot."

In 1772, Warren was appointed to the Boston Committee of Correspondence. The committee was designed to draft protests, which were sent to Parliament, as well as published in the colonies, in order to set forth the colonial arguments.

In September 1774, Warren drafted a set of resolutions, the Suffolk Resolves, which called for the British to repeal the provisions of the Intolerable Acts. Local representatives from Suffolk County, Massachusetts, adopted the resolutions. The resolves were delivered by Paul Revere to the Continental Congress in Philadelphia. The Congress endorsed the resolves on September 17.

It was natural that, on May 31, 1775, Warren was the choice of the leaders of Boston as president pro tempore of the Massachusetts Provincial Congress. His leadership qualities also caused the Provincial Congress to name him a major general in the Massachusetts colonial militia. It was while exercising this command that Warren became the first prominent causality of the American Revolution. That unfortunate event occurred during the Battle of Bunker Hill, which was actually fought on Breed's Hill.

In May 1775, General Gage, commanding the British forces in Boston, obtained reinforcements, which brought his total number of men to 6,500. The size of the British force caused Gage and his assistant generals to move to drive the American rebels from positions where they commanded the heights about the harbor.

The colonials under Warren had anticipated such a possibility, however, and on June 16, 1775, the Americans occupied Breed's Hill, which overlooked Boston Harbor from the north. On the following morning, Gage decided to make a frontal attack on the American positions, with the actual field command of the British forces to be placed with General Howe.

The 2,200 British soldiers formed up to make the attack were ferried from Boston to the Charlestown isthmus, upon which Breed's Hill was located. On a hot June day, the British moved up the hill with heavy packs, and the slowness of their ascent allowed the Americans to hold their fire until it could be most effective. When the British forces were within fifty yards of the American lines, Warren's men opened fire. Twice the British were driven down the hill. During the third attack, the Americans ran out of powder and were forced to flee. It was during the third attack on Breed's Hill that General Warren was killed. Warren, a physician and patriot, was exceedingly popular in Boston, and his death was followed by a considerable amount of public mourning.

American Leaders & Innovators: Colonial Times to Reconstruction   Joseph Warren

Name: _____ Date: _____

Recalling Key Details

1. How did Joseph Warren receive his training as a physician?

2. What caused Warren to turn to revolutionary activities?

3. What action did Warren take to oppose the Townshend Acts?

4. What was the purpose of the Committee of Correspondence?

5. What is the meaning of the word *resolves* as it is used in paragraph four of the reading selection?

6. What were the Suffolk Resolves?

7. How did Joseph Warren use his writing skills to promote revolutionary activities?

American Leaders & Innovators: Colonial Times to Reconstruction   Joseph Warren

Name: _____   Date: _____

Activity

Directions: Research the connection between Joseph Warren and each Revolutionary War event. Write the connection in the box.

April 18, 1775

Famous ride of Paul Revere and William Dawes

Connection

April 19, 1775

Battle of Lexington and Concord

Connection

May 10, 1775

Capture of Fort Ticonderoga by Ethan Allen and Benedict Arnold

Connection

John Jay 1745–1829

READING SELECTION

John Jay, born in 1745, was educated by private tutors before he entered King's College in New York, where he developed his skills as a writer. Jay was admitted to the New York Bar in 1768 and went on to become a successful lawyer.

When the American Revolution began in 1776, the Continental Congress needed diplomats abroad. Jay gave up his successful law practice to serve his country. He was sent to Spain to get support for American independence. Unsuccessful, he joined Benjamin Franklin, John Adams, and Henry Laurens in Paris, France, and helped to negotiate the treaty that would end the war. In 1783, the Treaty of Paris was signed, giving the colonies independence from Great Britain.

At the end of the Revolution, Spain closed the Mississippi River to American trade, an act calculated to cause problems on the frontier. Jay, as the American "secretary of state," tried to solve the situation by conceding some territorial claims in the West. The Congress under the Articles of Confederation refused to go along with this, however, and for a while, Jay suffered from public rebuke.

Problems arose when the Revolutionary War ended. The Articles of Confederation did not allow the national government to raise taxes, regulate trade or settle disputes between the states, or to deal with foreign governments. A convention was called to discuss revising the Articles of Confederation.

In 1787, 55 delegates gathered in Philadelphia for the Constitutional Convention. They decided to write a new constitution. After the Convention, people known as Federalists began speaking out in favor of ratifying the new Constitution. Anti-Federalists such as Patrick Henry and James Monroe spoke out in opposition, believing it gave too much power to the national government and not enough power to the states. They wanted a Bill of Rights added to the document in order to guarantee the protection of the rights of the people. Federalists wanted a strong federal government. They argued a Bill of Rights wasn't needed because the Constitution limited the power of the federal government.

Jay, along with Alexander Hamilton and James Madison, campaigned vigorously for public acceptance of the new government. Beginning in 1787, the three men wrote 85 essays in various newspapers, promoting the Constitution. The collection of essays is known as *The Federalist Papers*. In order to get the Constitution ratified by the states, the Federalists finally promised to add a Bill of Rights to the Constitution. *The Federalist Papers* were a major factor in winning ratification of the Constitution.

Possibly as a reward for his work in winning the public over to the new government, Jay was appointed Chief Justice of the Supreme Court. In that office, he was constantly consulted by President Washington. It was Jay who wrote the first draft of the Proclamation of Neutrality of 1793, declaring the nation neutral in any conflicts between France and Great Britain. The United States tried to stay out of the European conflict, but the country became subject to various aggressions by France and England. To avoid war, Washington sent Jay to London in order to negotiate a treaty. Jay's Treaty, as it was called, won few concessions from the British and, in fact, became the subject of public uproar. In the end, however, the treaty did serve to keep the United States out of war for a number of years.

Jay negotiated peace treaties, worked to ratify the Constitution, and served as the first Chief Justice of the Supreme Court. These contributions ensure his place in American history.

American Leaders & Innovators: Colonial Times to Reconstruction — John Jay

Name: _____ Date: _____

Recalling Key Details

1. What did the Treaty of Paris accomplish?

2. Who were the four Americans who negotiated the Treaty of Paris?

3. What is the meaning of the word **Federalists** as it is used in paragraph five of the reading selection?

4. What were *The Federalist Papers*?

5. Who were the three men who wrote *The Federalist Papers*?

6. What was the purpose of the 1793 Proclamation of Neutrality?

7. What was John Jay's major contribution to the establishment of the new government under the Constitution?

American Leaders & Innovators: Colonial Times to Reconstruction — John Jay

Name: _____ Date: _____

Activity

Directions: Research the Federalist movement. Use the information to write a newspaper article explaining the public relations campaign waged by the Federalists to promote ratification of the United States Constitution.

Writing a News Article

The purpose of a news article is to inform readers of facts and information about events. Journalists use the inverted pyramid structure when writing news articles.

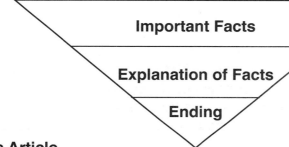

Elements of a News Article

1. **Headline:** A short attention-grabbing phrase that presents the main idea of the article.
2. **Byline:** Tells who wrote the article.
3. **Lead Paragraph (Introduction):** All the important information is revealed in the opening paragraph. It contains the answers to the important questions of the article:

   - Who is the article about?
   - What happened?
   - When did it happen?
   - Where did it happen?
   - Why did it happen?
   - How did it happen?

4. **Explanation:** Organized from the most to least important information, these paragraphs explain the story.
5. **Conclusion:** A paragraph that wraps up the article. It should be short and shouldn't include any new information.

How to Write a Great News Story

1. Tell the news story in a way that holds the reader's interest.
2. Include quotes made by people mentioned in the story.
3. Use text features and graphics to enhance the reader's understanding of information presented.
4. Include a caption or sentence explaining photographs or illustrations included in the article.
5. Make the story stick in the minds of the readers by writing a dynamite conclusion.

Tecumseh 1768–1813

READING SELECTION

Tecumseh was a Shawnee warrior and leader. He dedicated his life to uniting Native American tribes east of the Mississippi River to fight westward expansion into the Northwest Territory. Tecumseh was born in 1768 in what is now Ohio. He grew up during a time of almost constant conflict between the Shawnee and white settlers. In 1774, his father was killed by American soldiers during Lord Dunmore's War. The war between the Native Americans and settlers was fought over ownership of land in the Ohio Valley. Afterwards, his mother moved with part of the tribe to Missouri, leaving Tecumseh behind to be raised by his sister.

Tecumseh became an important leader while still a young man. He participated in many raids on white settlements and took part in several battles, including the Battle of Fallen Timbers in 1794. A victory for the United States, the battle ended the Northwest Indian War. In 1795, the Treaty of Greenville was signed. Tecumseh disputed the treaty over the surrender of tribal lands and refused to sign.

Tecumseh met with considerable success in his efforts to unite the tribes against the settlers. His brother, Tenskwatawa, called the "Shawnee Prophet," greatly aided Tecumseh in his efforts. The name "Prophet" was given to Tenskwatawa because he had once overheard British officers discussing the fact that an eclipse of the sun was due on a certain date. He returned to his tribe and told his people that, at a certain time, the sun would die and then later return. After this event, he was known as the Prophet.

Tecumseh, his brother, and some members of his tribe left the Ohio area around 1808. They went to the Indiana Territory close to where the Tippecanoe and Wabash Rivers joined and founded the village of Prophetstown.

In 1809, William Henry Harrison, governor of the Indiana Territory, convinced several tribal leaders to sign the Treaty of Fort Wayne. The treaty gave to the United States three million acres of Native American land. Tecumseh opposed the treaty, questioning whether the leaders had the authority to sell the land. Tecumseh then began recruiting tribes to join his newly formed confederation to fight expansion of the United States. His goal was to form an independent nation of Native Americans east of the Mississippi. A gifted speaker, Tecumseh traveled constantly in an effort to convince the tribes to unite.

In 1811, Governor William Henry Harrison, concerned with the alliances formed by Tecumseh, attacked Prophetstown at Tippecanoe while Tecumseh was away recruiting. At the Battle of Tippecanoe, Harrison destroyed their village and various supplies. The Native Americans withdrew after the battle and left behind guns with English markings on them. To American westerners, this was proof that the Native Americans were being armed by the British.

During the War of 1812, Tecumseh and his followers joined the British against the United States. He served as a brigadier general with the British. He hoped to get the British to help halt the American advance into the Northwest.

In 1813, Harrison got his troops across Lake Erie and fought both Native Americans and British on the Thames River. In this affair, the Battle of the Thames, Tecumseh was killed by an American officer named Richard Johnson. Harrison used the fame of his victories to move eventually into the White House; Johnson used his own wartime reputation to vault into the vice-presidency.

Recalling Key Details

1. Who was Tecumseh?

2. Why did Tecumseh want to form a confederacy of tribes?

3. What ability did Tecumseh possess that enabled him to unite Native Americans in the Northwest Territory?

4. What does the word *treaty* mean as it is used in paragraph five of the reading selection?

5. Why did William Henry Harrison send troops to Prophetstown?

6. How was it revealed that the British were helping the Native Americans?

7. What actions did Tecumseh take to prevent the expansion of the United States into tribal lands?

Activity

Directions: Use information from the reading selection to develop a timeline identifying the major events in the life of Tecumseh. Follow the steps below to create your timeline.

> **Materials:**
> 5" x 8" index cards, unlined   clear tape
> yarn   markers
> colored pencils   pen or pencil

Step 1: Review the reading selection. Select the major events in the life of Tecumseh.

Step 2: Record the information for each event on an index card. At the top of each card, sketch a picture or glue a graphic to illustrate the event. Below the illustration, write the date the event occurred. At the bottom of the card, write a brief description of the event.

Step 3: Organize the cards in chronological order from earliest to latest date.

Step 4: Cut a piece of yarn two yards long. Tape the organized cards to the string. Leave enough string on both ends for displaying.

1768

Tecumseh was born into the Shawnee tribe.

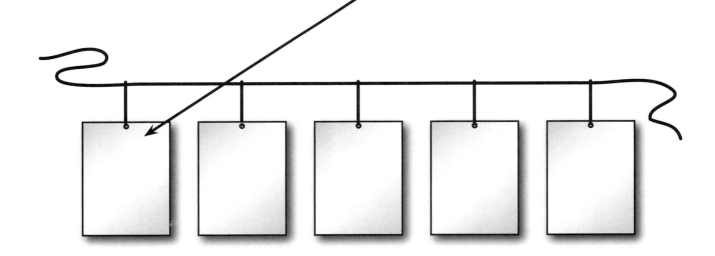

Dolley Madison 1768–1849

READING SELECTION

Dolley Madison was born in Guilford County, North Carolina, in 1768. She spent part of her childhood in Scotchtown, Virginia. In 1783, the year the American Revolution ended, she and her family moved to Philadelphia. Several years later, in 1790, she married John Todd, Jr., who was a Quaker lawyer. By this marriage she bore two sons. In 1793, both her husband and one of her sons died. A year later, she married James Madison who, at the time of the marriage, was a congressman from Virginia.

Dolley's new husband was a remarkable man. Throughout the Revolutionary period, James Madison played an important role. James, along with Alexander Hamilton, helped to guide the course of the Constitutional Convention of 1787. When the Constitution was finished, both Madison and Hamilton helped write *The Federalist Papers* in order to persuade a nationwide acceptance of the Constitution.

Courtesy of the University of Texas Libraries, The University of Texas at Austin

Four years after James' marriage to Dolley, both the Virginia statesman and his wife retired to Montpelier, Madison's plantation in Orange County, Virginia. In 1801, however, President Jefferson appointed Madison to the office of secretary of state, and from that position Madison vaulted into the presidency.

In 1809, James Madison became the fourth President of the United States. When the Madisons moved into the presidential mansion, which had been under construction since President Washington, the interior was not complete. Dolley worked with the architect Benjamin Henry Latrobe to decorate and furnish the mansion, making it the center of social gatherings in Washington, D.C. She was known for her charm and social grace as a hostess, which became a great asset for President Madison. The term "First Lady" originated with Dolley Madison.

Madison's first term was a hectic time. On several occasions, war was narrowly averted by the young nation. Finally, in 1812, through a combination of events, Congress voted for, and Madison signed, a declaration of war against Great Britain. This became known as the War of 1812. During the war, the British landed in Chesapeake Bay, beat some hastily gathered American forces at Blandensburg, and then marched to Washington, the capital city. British soldiers burned most of the city; it has been said that when the invaders entered the president's house, they found a still-warm meal that had been hastily left by the president and his wife.

Dolley Madison apparently was the last person to leave the president's house prior to the British entry into Washington. She managed to save a famous painting of President Washington by cutting it from its frame, and she also saved a number of very valuable presidential papers. Upon returning to Washington, she found a blackened presidential mansion that would need to be rebuilt.

James and Dolley returned to Montpelier in 1817, where he lived until his death in 1836. Dolley returned to Washington in her later years and lived there until her death in 1849. For her contributions to American history, she was honored with a commemorative postage stamp in 1980 and a silver dollar minted in 1999.

American Leaders & Innovators: Colonial Times to Reconstruction — Dolley Madison

Name: _____   Date: _____

Recalling Key Details

1. Where was Dolley Madison born?

2. When did James and Dolley Madison move into the presidential mansion?

3. What role did Dolley Madison play in making the president's house the center of Washington, D.C., society?

4. What characteristics did Dolley Madison possess that contributed to her husband's presidential success?

5. What does the title **First Lady** mean as it is used in paragraph four of the reading selection?

6. In which war did the British burn the presidential mansion?

7. What was Dolley Madison's greatest contribution as "First Lady" of the United States?

American Leaders & Innovators: Colonial Times to Reconstruction — Dolley Madison

Name: _____ Date: _____

Activity

Directions: Create a postcard about Dolley Madison. On the front of your postcard include a graphic or sketch that illustrates an important event in her life. On the back of the card write a brief description explaining the illustration and an important fact about her life as First Lady. Cut out the completed postcard. Fold the card in half and tape or glue the sides together.

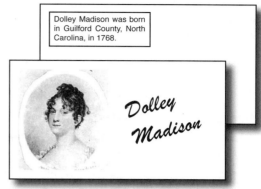

Description:

Fact:

Winfield Scott 1786–1866

READING SELECTION

Winfield Scott was an army officer for over 50 years. He served in three major wars: the War of 1812, the Mexican War, and the Civil War.

Scott was born on June 13, 1786, in Virginia, not far from the very spot at which Robert E. Lee surrendered to General Grant in 1865. He studied at William and Mary College, with the idea of practicing law. That course of life bored him, and in 1808, he joined the United States Army. When the War of 1812 broke out, Scott was made a lieutenant colonel and sent to the Canadian border. He was captured at the Battle of Queenston Heights on October 13, 1812, but was later exchanged by the British.

Scott was a natural for army command from the beginning, and he soon attained the rank of colonel. He carried out a successful campaign to clear the banks of the Niagara River during the War of 1812, which allowed Oliver H. Perry to get his small fleet into Lake Erie. Soon, as a brigadier general, Scott fought two bitter battles—at Chippewa on July 5, 1814, and at Lundy's Lane on July 25, 1814. He was wounded at Lundy's Lane and carried from the battlefield.

Now a national hero, Scott was awarded a Congressional Gold Medal in 1814. Although the war ended in 1815, Scott stayed with the army and was promoted to the rank of major general. At that time, he composed *Rules and Regulations for the Field Exercise and Maneuvers of Infantry*, the manual of arms for organizing and training the U.S. Army. The manual continued to be used through the Civil War.

In 1841, Scott was made the general-in-chief of the army. Scott did such a good job training the army that when the Mexican War broke out, American soldiers performed magnificently. He led one of the American armies in the campaign, and his strong discipline earned him the name of "Old Fuss and Feathers." Despite the implications of the title, Scott's men suffered less from disease and hardship than any other command in Mexico.

Scott's invasion of Mexico was one of the greatest campaigns of all time. He landed at Vera Cruz on the Mexican coast and marched into the heart of Mexico. There followed a series of battles—Cerro Gordo, Contreras, Churubusco, Molino del Rey, and Chapultepec. Mexico City was finally taken, after a valiant defense by the Mexican army. Once Scott captured the Mexican capital, he governed it with such justice that some Mexicans wished him to stay and become emperor of the country. After the war ended in 1848, Congress awarded Scott another Congressional Gold Medal for his outstanding leadership in the war.

In the presidential election of 1852, Scott ran as the Whig Party candidate against Franklin Pierce, the Democratic candidate. Pierce, who had been wounded in Mexico as a volunteer general, had the advantage. He had a united Democratic Party and was already a politician, while Scott had some of the characteristics of a crusty career general.

With the onset of the Civil War, Scott, who was still in charge of the army, was faced with a dilemma. He was a Virginian, and that state had seceded from the Union. Scott stayed with the Union, however, and organized its forces in 1861. He even devised the Anaconda Plan, which was later applied by President Lincoln against the South. But Scott was 74 years old and tired. He was no longer able to operate a field command. In November 1861, Scott retired from the army. Scott died on May 29, 1866, at West Point, New York. He had lived long enough to see a Union victory.

American Leaders & Innovators: Colonial Times to Reconstruction — Winfield Scott

Name: _____ Date: _____

Recalling Key Details

1. In what three major wars did Winfield Scott serve?

2. What was the importance of the Niagara River campaign during the War of 1812?

3. What was the importance of the manual of arms for the U.S. Army?

4. Why did some Mexican citizens want Scott to become emperor of Mexico?

5. Why did Franklin Pierce have a greater advantage than Scott in the presidential campaign of 1852?

6. What is the meaning of the word **seceded** as it is used in the last paragraph of the reading selection?

7. What were Winfield Scott's major accomplishments as a military officer?

American Leaders & Innovators: Colonial Times to Reconstruction   Winfield Scott

Name: _____ Date: _____

Activity

In 1861, General Winfield Scott devised a strategy for Union forces to defeat the Confederacy. This plan would later become known as the **Anaconda Plan**.

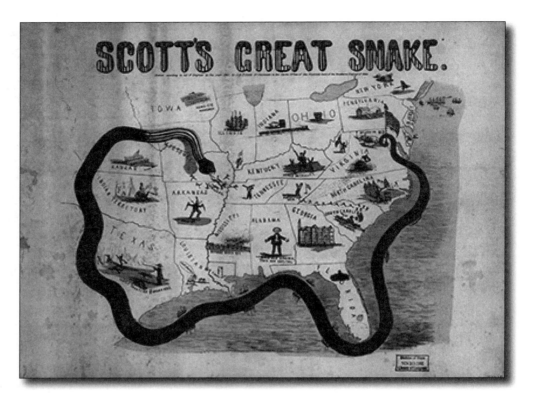

Directions: Research the Anaconda Plan. Explain the plan's two major objectives.

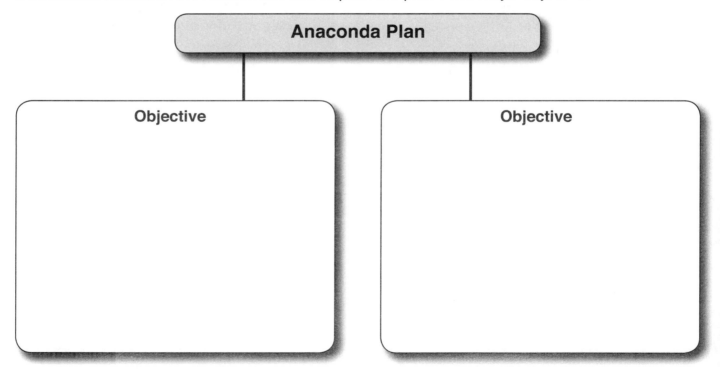

Benjamin Lundy 1789–1839

READING SELECTION

Benjamin Lundy was a publisher and an outspoken opponent of slavery in the years before the American Civil War. An abolitionist, he called for the "immediate and complete emancipation" of slaves.

Lundy was born in Sussex County, New Jersey, to Quaker parents. Quakers were especially active in the anti-slavery movement. Benjamin was given only the barest formal education. At the age of nineteen, he chose to enter the saddler's trade. To learn this trade, he went to Virginia where he first came into contact with slavery.

In 1815, he was in Ohio, where he organized the Union Humane Society, an anti-slavery association. He was so taken with the goals of abolitionism that he contributed articles to various anti-slavery publications. In 1821, Lundy began the publication of his own newspaper, *The Genius of Universal Emancipation*. *The Genius* was the forerunner of most influential abolitionist newspapers. Lundy had trouble finding a location in which to publish the newspaper since he was forever meeting opposition. By 1824, he had established his press in Baltimore, Maryland.

Benjamin Lundy was a pioneer of the anti-slavery movement.

Lundy apparently did not merely want to abolish slavery, but he also became intensely interested in the American Colonization Society's plan for the recolonization of former slaves to Africa. He went to Haiti numerous times in order to find other suitable places in which to colonize African Americans—each trip resulting in failure.

By this time, Lundy was attracting the interest of pro-slavery groups, and in 1827, he was physically assaulted by a Baltimore slaver as a result of his newspaper's position on slavery. A year later, Lundy took his crusade to the various northern states in order to curry support. During this trip, he gained the active support of William Lloyd Garrison, a New Englander who joined Lundy in the publication of *The Genius*. But Garrison was so aggressive in his writing that numerous lawsuits were brought against Lundy and his paper, and as a result, he and Garrison soon parted ways.

By the mid-1830s, Lundy was living in Philadelphia, where he began the publication of another activist newspaper. His most notable effort during this time was the publication of a pamphlet called *The War in Texas*. Lundy opposed the annexation of Texas and did it so vigorously that he may have been one of the factors in delaying the statehood of Texas.

By this time, he had so many enemies in Pennsylvania that his life was in danger. His personal papers and equipment were burned by mobs, forcing him to leave Pennsylvania. He traveled through various parts of the West, helping to organize anti-slavery societies. During this last phase of his life, a few more issues of *The Genius* were published.

Lundy died in 1839, before the abolitionist movement really began to threaten the institution of slavery in a serious way. It must be said, however, that he was a noble pioneer in an attempt to point out the wrongs of slavery.

American Leaders & Innovators: Colonial Times to Reconstruction — Benjamin Lundy

Name: _____ Date: _____

Recalling Key Details

1. What does the word **abolitionist** mean as it is used in the first paragraph of the reading selection?

2. How did Benjamin Lundy's Quaker beliefs shape his views on slavery?

3. What was the name of the anti-slavery newspaper established by Lundy?

4. What did Lundy have in common with the American Colonization Society?

5. Who helped Lundy with the publication of *The Genius*? Why?

6. Why did Lundy publish the pamphlet *The War in Texas*?

7. How did Benjamin Lundy help promote the abolitionist movement in the United States?

American Leaders & Innovators: Colonial Times to Reconstruction   Benjamin Lundy

Name: _____   Date: _____

Activity

Directions: Create a bookmark about Benjamin Lundy. Use information from the reading selection to fill in the details. Cut out the bookmark and glue it to sturdy cardstock. Punch a hole at the top. Run yarn through the hole and tie. On the back side of the bookmark, create an illustration that honors Lundy's life as an American hero.

Benjamin Lundy

Interesting Fact

_____
_____
_____
_____

Famous Quote

_____
_____
_____
_____

Major Accomplishment

_____
_____
_____
_____

Name: _____

David Glasgow Farragut 1801–1870

READING SELECTION

James "David" Glasgow Farragut was born near Knoxville, Tennessee, in 1801. His father, Jorge, was a Spanish merchant captain who had served in both the American Revolution and the War of 1812. James went to sea before he was ten—in fact, he took the name of David after his adoption by the noted naval officer Captain David Porter. Young Farragut served under Porter as a midshipman during the battle between the USS *Essex* and HMS *Phoebe* and *Cherub* in the War of 1812. After a long career in the U.S. Navy, Farragut became a captain in 1855.

His first important action during the Civil War took place in the West. In command of seagoing combat ships, he ordered the bombardment of Vicksburg, Mississippi, in 1862. He had managed to bring these larger vessels past the Confederate forts at New Orleans by the daring maneuver of sailing past the enemy batteries.

David Farragut was the first U.S. naval officer to hold the titles of rear admiral, admiral, and vice admiral.

Later, Farragut was annoyed by the failure of the Union government to order him against Mobile, Alabama, a major Confederate stronghold. Farragut had felt that the expedition would have been successful as early as 1862; but unfortunately, as sometimes happens in war, the national government seemed overcome by the magnitude of its problems. In January of 1864, Farragut became so despondent at the lack of direction in naval strategy that he wrote: "I am depressed by the bad news from every direction." Merely patrolling outside the entrance to Mobile Bay was not Farragut's idea of warfare.

Finally, in August of 1864, Farragut received the orders he had been waiting for. "I am going into Mobile in the morning, if God is my leader," Farragut wrote his wife. On the morning of August 5, Farragut, now an admiral, told the captain of the *Hartford*, "Well, Drayton, we might as well get under way." His fleet, which consisted of four monitors (iron-clad ships) and 14 wooden vessels, sailed directly for the entrance of Mobile Bay, which was lined with torpedoes.

Soon the leading monitor, the *Tecumseh*, was sunk by a torpedo. The *Hartford*, with Farragut lashed to the rigging, took the lead. The fleet commander had resorted to this action in order to see over the smoke of battle. It is during this episode in the Battle of Mobile Bay that Farragut was supposed to have said, "Damn the torpedoes! Four bells!"—a signal for full speed ahead.

Within three hours, Farragut defeated Admiral Franklin Buchanan and the Confederate ships in the harbor. Mobile Bay and the harbor were now under Union control. By capturing the last open seaport on the Gulf of Mexico, Farragut was now a Union hero.

The city of Mobile remained Confederate, but after the defeat of General Hood at Nashville, Tennessee, in 1865, Union forces moved freely into the Gulf region. General E.R.S. Canby finally took his Union troops into Mobile, the last major Confederate fortress to surrender.

Farragut was a leading naval hero of the Union in the war. In 1866, Farragut was promoted to the rank of rear admiral, a rank never before used in the U.S. Navy. The promotion made him the highest ranking Hispanic to serve in the Civil War.

American Leaders & Innovators: Colonial Times to Reconstruction   David Glasgow Farragut

Name: _____ Date: _____

Recalling Key Details

1. Which naval officer did David Glasgow Farragut serve under as a midshipman?

2. In which war did Farragut see his first naval action?

3. Which side did Farragut serve on during the Civil War?

4. Why was Farragut annoyed with the Union government?

5. What does the word **vessels** mean as used in paragraph four of the reading selection?

6. In which battle is Farragut reported to have shouted, "Damn the torpedoes! Four bells!"

7. What contribution did David Glasgow Farragut make as a Union naval officer during the Civil War?

American Leaders & Innovators: Colonial Times to Reconstruction — David Glasgow Farragut

Name: _____   Date: _____

Activity

A museum brochure provides visitors with information about the collection of artifacts and other objects of importance on display. A well-planned and designed brochure includes information of interest to tourists.

Directions: Examine a variety of brochures. Look closely at how graphics, text structures, and print features support the information contained in the brochures. Create a tri-fold brochure featuring the life of Civil War hero David Glasgow Farragut. Make sure the brochure includes well-organized information, easy-to-read font, print features that enhance the text, and appropriate graphics.

How to Make a Tri-fold Brochure

A tri-fold brochure is a single sheet of paper printed on both sides and folded into thirds. After folding, there are six panels for information (three panels on the outside and three panels on the inside). Each panel contains factual information about the topic. Graphics support the information presented in the brochure. A variety of print features are used to help the reader more easily navigate the text.

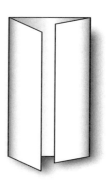

Outside Brochure

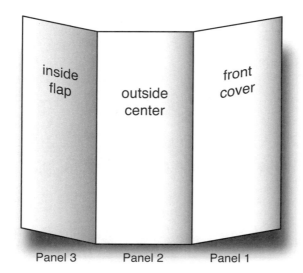

Panel 3 — inside flap
Panel 2 — outside center
Panel 1 — front cover

Inside Brochure

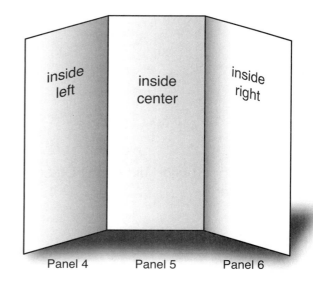

Panel 4 — inside left
Panel 5 — inside center
Panel 6 — inside right

Dorothea Lynde Dix 1802–1887

READING SELECTION

Dorothea Lynde Dix was born in Hampden, Maine, on April 4, 1802. When she was 12 years old, she moved to Worcester, Massachusetts, to live with her wealthy grandmother. Early in her life, she was afflicted with a form of tuberculosis. From then on, she lived her life as a semi-invalid who required long periods of recuperation. Yet, in spite of this, she worked tirelessly for the causes in which she believed. Between 1816 and 1836, she sporadically operated schools for girls or taught classes from her home. When her health would not allow her to teach, she would write. Her first book *Conversations of Common Things,* a reader for children, was published in 1824.

In 1836, Dix traveled to England in an effort to restore her health. While there, she became acquainted with social reformers working on changing prison conditions and the treatment of the mentally ill. It was during this time she decided upon the kind of work to which she would devote her life.

Dorothea Lynde Dix was a social reformer in the 19th century.

In 1841, Dix began teaching Sunday School classes to women in the East Cambridge Jail. She determined that conditions in the women's prison had to be changed and the treatment of the mentally ill had to be humanized. She asked Dr. Samuel Gridley Howe, a physician and social reformer, for his advice on what she could do to bring about change. Dr. Howe urged Dix to undertake a three-year investigation of the treatment of the mentally ill.

In 1843, at the end of her investigation into the conditions in Massachusetts, she wrote a *Memorial to the Legislature of Massachusetts.* In it she stated: "I come to present the strong claims of suffering humanity…to call your attention to the present state of insane persons confined within this Commonwealth, in cages, closets, cellars, stalls, pens! Chained, naked, beaten with rods, and lashed into obedience."

By 1845, Dix had traveled 10,000 miles, visited 300 jails and houses of correction, 500 almshouses, and 18 state prisons, researching the plight of the mentally ill. Through her efforts, forms of relief were given to the mentally ill. No longer were they kept in prisons along with criminals, but states throughout the nation built asylums for their treatment. From everywhere came support from other reformers and philanthropists. Twenty states and Canada moved to adopt most of her suggestions.

But Dix was not yet finished. In 1854, she revisited England, which had similarly bad conditions in its treatment of the mentally ill. She added her voice to the cries of reform there, and changes were eventually made. She traveled throughout much of Europe speaking about the need for reform, and wherever she went, she found people who listened.

When the American Civil War broke out in 1861, Dix volunteered her services, and she was appointed as the Superintendent of Army Nurses. Her job was to recruit, train, and organize female nurses for the Union Army. She was exceedingly strict in the administration of rules over these nurses, but her efforts won for female nurses the thanks of a grateful nation.

Dorothea Lynde Dix never married. Despite her periodic bouts with tuberculosis, she lived until 1887—a span of 85 years. She died on July 10, 1887, in Trenton, New Jersey.

American Leaders & Innovators: Colonial Times to Reconstruction   Dorothea Lynde Dix

Name: _____ Date: _____

Recalling Key Details

1. What was Dorothea Lynde Dix's primary occupation before becoming a social reformer?

2. What was the outcome of Dix's trip to England in 1836?

3. What is the meaning of the word **reformers** as it is used in paragraph two of the reading selection?

4. What did Dix's 1843 report reveal about the care and treatment of the mentally ill?

5. What changes in the treatment of the mentally ill occurred as a result of the reform efforts of Dix?

6. What were Dix's duties as Superintendent of Army Nurses?

7. What contributions did Dorothea Lynde Dix make as a social reformer?

American Leaders & Innovators: Colonial Times to Reconstruction — Dorothea Lynde Dix

Name: _____ Date: _____

Activity

Directions: Cut out the Social Reformers of the 1800s flap chart below. Cut on the solid lines to create ten flaps. Apply glue to the back of the title tab and attach the flap chart to a separate sheet of paper. Research each person. Under each flap, write a brief description of the person's contribution to social reform.

Social Reformers of the 1800s

- Jane Addams
- Dorothea Lynde Dix
- Frederick Douglass
- William Lloyd Garrison
- Julia Ward Howe
- Helen Hunt Jackson
- Horace Mann
- Lucretia Mott
- Sojourner Truth
- Frances Willard

Justin Smith Morrill 1810–1898

READING SELECTION

Justin Smith Morrill was one of the most important factors in American growth in the nineteenth century. His contributions to higher education still impact colleges and universities today.

Justin Morrill, the son of a blacksmith, was born on April 14, 1810, in Strafford, Vermont. He was educated at the village school and local academies. At fifteen years of age, he became a store clerk, an occupation which he followed until 1828. Soon, he was a partner in a local store and gained so much wealth from business investments that he was able to retire in 1848 at a young age.

After marrying in 1851, Morrill entered into local politics with zeal. He served on county and state committees, and in 1852, he attended the Whig convention as a delegate. In 1854, Morrill entered Congress as one of the few remaining members of the dying Whig Party. Later, Morrill joined the newly formed Republican Party.

Justin Morrill served almost 44 years in Congress.

Morrill's life constituted a long record of public service. He represented his Vermont constituents for six terms in the House, and in 1866, he was elected to the Senate, where he served for almost 32 years.

His committee assignments were varied and important. He was a member of the Ways and Means Committee, served as Chairman of the Committee on Finance, and pushed the principle of abolition. As a member of the Ways and Means Committee, Morrill wrote a bill that eventually became known as the Morrill Tariff Act. The act increased import taxes on goods imported into the United States.

His greatest accomplishment was the famous Land-Grant College Act (Morrill Act) signed by President Lincoln in 1862. The act provided a federal land grant equal to 30,000 acres to every state for each senator or representative it was entitled to under the census of 1860. In other words, if a state was entitled to two representatives and two senators, then it would receive 120,000 acres. The income resulting from the sale of these lands by each state was to be used to endow, support, and maintain at least one college where the leading objective was the teaching of agriculture and mechanic arts.

Western states were the first to accept public lands for educational purposes. State universities were created in Kansas (1863), Illinois (1867), Minnesota (1868), and California (1868). One of the earlier eastern schools to accept public funds on the basis of the Morrill Act was Cornell University.

In 1890, Morrill pushed through the Second Morrill Act to increase the amount of money available to land-grant schools. The act also led to the establishment of African-American land-grant colleges and universities. He was also responsible for the beautification of Washington, D.C., in the 1890s. Justin Smith Morrill died in Washington, D.C., on December 28, 1898. At the time of his death, he had served almost 44 years in Congress.

The old "land-grant" universities have served the country well, both in providing education for the masses and in developing new techniques in industry, farming, and commerce. Agriculture alone has been revolutionized through innovations and discoveries made at these universities.

Recalling Key Details

1. How did Justin Smith Morrill acquire his wealth?

2. Why did Morrill join the Republican Party?

3. What is the meaning of the word *delegate* as it is used in paragraph three of the reading selection?

4. What was the purpose of the Tariff Act written by Morrill?

5. How many years did Morrill serve as a U.S. senator?

6. In which state was the first land grant university established?

7. What was Justin Smith Morrill's greatest accomplishment as a U.S. representative and senator?

American Leaders & Innovators: Colonial Times to Reconstruction Justin Smith Morrill

Name: _____ Date: _____

Activity

Directions: Research the Hatch Act of 1887, the Second Morrill Act of 1890, the Smith-Lever Act of 1914, and the Land-Grant Status Act of 1994. Use the directions below to create a four-shutter window foldable.

1. Fold a full sheet of paper into quarters, then open it back up.

2. Turn the paper lengthwise. Fold one side of the paper toward the center fold line to make a flap. Repeat on the other side to make a second flap. Then cut each flap in half. You now have four shutter windows.

3. Cut apart the four boxes below and attach one to the front of each window flap. Under each flap, write the purpose of the Act.

Hatch Act of 1887	Second Morrill Act of 1890
Smith-Lever Act of 1914	Land-Grant Status Act of 1994

CD-405034 © Mark Twain Media, Inc., Publishers

Harriet Beecher Stowe 1811–1896

> **READING SELECTION**

Readers laughed at Topsy's humor, trembled as Eliza escaped, and wept when Uncle Tom died. These people were imaginary, but to readers, they were real. For the first time, many began to see slaves as real people suffering terrible injustices. No novel had ever stirred such a response. The success of *Uncle Tom's Cabin* exceeded any ambition of its author, Harriet Beecher Stowe, and its effect stirred world opinion.

Harriet Beecher Stowe was born June 14, 1811, in Litchfield, Connecticut. Stowe came from a family of famous ministers. Her father, Lyman Beecher, was a man of strong opinions. Her favorite brother, Henry Ward Beecher, became the most famous minister in the country. She married Calvin Stowe, a minister and professor at Lane Theological Seminary in Cincinnati where her father was president. To add to her husband's small salary, she wrote short stories whenever she could. However, with seven children, she was very busy.

Harriet Beecher Stowe was the author of over 30 books.

The family often discussed slavery. To them, it was a social sin and not an individual sin. The slave owner was caught up in the "evil system" of slavery. Stowe met runaway slaves, and they told her about the terrible conditions they escaped. Thoughts of slavery tormented her.

In 1850, she and her husband moved to Maine where Professor Stowe taught at Bowdoin College. While visiting with her brother Edward, they talked about the Compromise of 1850, which they both opposed. Her sister-in-law wrote Harriet: "If I could just use the pen as you can, I would write something that would make this whole nation feel what an accursed thing slavery is." Stowe answered that she could do little writing because of the baby, "But I will do it at last. I will write the thing if I live."

As she sat in church one gloomy Sunday, images crossed her mind. She saw a black man being whipped and the dying man asking God's forgiveness for those who had beaten him. She thought of escaped slaves she had met in Cincinnati and their stories. She rushed home and began to write, and when she ran out of writing paper, she wrote on a grocery sack.

The story was first published in serial form in *National Era,* an abolitionist newspaper in June 1851. Then the completed story was published in book form in 1852. The book was an instant bestseller. It sold 300,000 copies in its first year in the United States and 1.5 million copies later in England. It was translated into over 60 languages.

When Stowe visited the White House in 1862, President Lincoln supposedly greeted her with the words: "Why Mrs. Stowe, I'm right glad to see you! So you're the little lady who wrote the book that made this great war?" *Uncle Tom's Cabin* may not have started the Civil War, but it brought the issue of slavery out in the open as never before.

Harriet Beecher Stowe continued to write after the success of *Uncle Tom's Cabin*. She published *Dred* in 1856, *The Minister's Wooing* in 1859, and *Old Town Folks* in 1869. She died in Hartford, Connecticut, in 1896.

Name: _____ Date: _____

Recalling Key Details

1. What is the meaning of the word *injustices* as it is used in the first paragraph of the reading selection?

2. How did Harriet Beecher Stowe's family view slavery?

3. What was Harriet Beecher Stowe's opinion on the Compromise of 1850?

4. Who encouraged Harriet Beecher Stowe to write a book about slavery?

5. What motivated Harriet Beecher Stowe to begin writing *Uncle Tom's Cabin*?

6. How successful was the book *Uncle Tom's Cabin*?

7. How did Harriet Beecher's Stowe's book *Uncle Tom's Cabin* change people's view of slavery?

Name: _____ Date: _____

Activity

Directions: Read Harriet Beecher Stowe's poem "Eliza Crossing the River." The poem is based on a scene from the book *Uncle Tom's Cabin.* Then answer the questions.

Eliza Crossing the River

From her resting-place by the trader chased,
Through the winter evening cold,
Eliza came with her boy at last,
Where a broad deep river rolled.

Great blocks of the floating ice were there,
And the water's roar was wild,
But the cruel trader's step was near,
Who would take her only child.

Poor Harry clung around her neck,
But a word he could not say,
For his very heart was faint with fear,
And with flying all that day.

Her arms about the boy grew tight,
With a loving clasp, and brave;
'Hold fast! Hold fast, now, Harry dear,
And it may be God will save.'

From the river's bank to the floating ice
She took a sudden bound,
And the great block swayed beneath her feet
With a dull and heavy sound.

So over the roaring rushing flood,
From block to block she sprang,
And ever her cry for God's good help
Above the waters rang.

And God did hear that mother's cry,
For never an ice-block sank;
While the cruel trader and his men
Stood wondering on the bank.

A good man saw on the further side,
And gave her his helping hand;
So poor Eliza, with her boy,
Stood safe upon the land.

A blessing on that good man's arm,
On his house, and field, and store;
May he never want a friendly hand
To help him to the shore!

A blessing on all that make such haste,
Whatever their hands can do!
For they that succor the sore distressed,
Our Lord will help them too.

1. What is the theme of the poem? _____
2. Why was Eliza willing to risk crossing the ice-filled river? _____
   _____
3. What is the meaning of the last three verses of the poem? _____
   _____
   _____

Elizabeth Cady Stanton 1815–1902

READING SELECTION

Elizabeth Cady Stanton was born on November 12, 1815, in Johnstown, New York. Her parents were wealthy; her father was a well-known lawyer and judge. One of the greatest influences in her young years was an elderly neighbor, Simon Hosack. A minister of the Presbyterian Church, he encouraged Elizabeth to pursue an education superior to that available to most girls of her time. Hosack tutored her in Greek, Latin, and mathematics. Later in life, she recounted that Hosack "cultivated in me a good deal of self-respect."

When Elizabeth was 15, she was sent to a girls' school operated by Emma Willard at Troy, New York. She graduated in 1832 and then entered into the study of law. She quickly learned that there were enormous handicaps for women who wanted a professional career. It was at this time that she became interested in both the temperance and anti-slavery movements.

In 1840, Elizabeth married Henry Brewster Stanton, and during the ceremony the word *obey* was omitted from the marriage vows. Stanton, an abolitionist leader, soon thereafter attended a world anti-slavery conference in London. Elizabeth went with him, and while there, met Lucretia Coffin Mott. Mrs. Mott and others were refused official recognition by the conference, and as a consequence, both Mrs. Mott and Mrs. Stanton determined to organize a women's rights convention.

The first women's rights convention was finally held in 1848, in the Wesleyan Methodist Church in Seneca Falls, New York. Many of the people who attended were also abolitionists whose goals included universal suffrage, the right of all people to vote regardless of sex, race, social status, or wealth. Through the insistence of Elizabeth Cady Stanton, a resolution calling for women's suffrage was adopted. From then on, a small group of women led the movement for the right to vote.

Stanton began to give more and more of her time to the cause of women's rights—lecturing, writing, and organizing local feminist groups. In 1851, she met Susan B. Anthony and persuaded her to enter the fight for women's rights. The two women were an ideal team. Elizabeth was the more skillful speaker, but Susan B. Anthony had more patience and organizational ability.

Stanton's aims covered the areas of divorce, suffrage, and professional rights. In 1869, she helped organize the National American Woman Suffrage Association and was consequently chosen as its first president. This was the most radical of women's organizations, and Stanton filled the presidency for 21 years.

Amazingly, Stanton was able to balance domestic demands with her personal goals. She bore seven children yet devoted eight months every year to lecturing throughout the states of the union. In 1868, she joined in the establishment of *Revolution*, a magazine devoted to women's rights. She also wrote for the *North American Review*.

In 1898, Elizabeth Cady Stanton published her own life story—*Eighty Years and More*. But even then, she was not quite finished. Along with Susan B. Anthony and Matilda Joslyn Gage, she helped to produce three enormous volumes of the *History of Woman Suffrage*. Stanton died in 1902. Sadly, she died before seeing the ratification of the Nineteenth Amendment in 1920, which gave women the right to vote.

American Leaders & Innovators: Colonial Times to Reconstruction   Elizabeth Cady Stanton

Name: _____ Date: _____

Recalling Key Details

1. What impact did Simon Hosack have on Elizabeth Cady Stanton's early education?

2. What career did Elizabeth Cady Stanton want to pursue after graduating in 1832?

3. What important role did Elizabeth Cady Stanton play at the Seneca Falls Convention in 1848?

4. After the convention, what actions did Elizabeth Cady Stanton take to advance the cause of women's rights?

5. What is the meaning of the phrase **universal suffrage** as it is used in paragraph four of the reading selection?

6. Why did Elizabeth Cady Stanton and Susan B. Anthony make the "ideal team"?

7. What contributions did Elizabeth Cady Stanton make to the advancement of women's rights?

Activity

Directions: Research the friendship between Elizabeth Cady Stanton and fellow suffragette, Susan B. Anthony. Write five interesting facts about their joint efforts to gain voting rights for women.

Fact:

Fact:

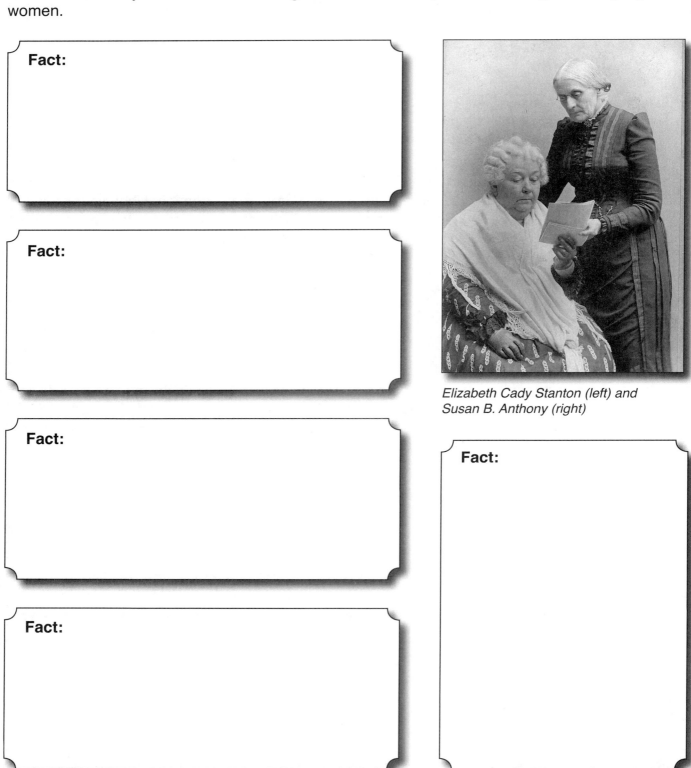

Elizabeth Cady Stanton (left) and Susan B. Anthony (right)

Fact:

Fact:

Fact:

Carl Schurz 1829–1906

READING SELECTION

Carl Schurz was born in Prussia and attended the University of Bonn. He was involved in the 1848 German revolutions, and after their failure, he and his wife immigrated to the United States in 1852. After settling in Wisconsin in 1855, he began to make his presence felt in the new land. Schurz studied law and was admitted to the Wisconsin Bar. He established his law practice in Milwaukee and soon became involved in the anti-slavery movement.

In 1860, Schurz worked hard on Lincoln's presidential campaign and was rewarded with an appointment as the U.S. Minister to Spain. In 1862, President Lincoln made him a brigadier general in the Union Army, and even though his military record was undistinguished, he managed to keep German-Americans strongly behind the cause.

Two months after the war ended in 1865, Schurz was sent by President Andrew Johnson to investigate conditions in some Southern states. Johnson wanted to know the effects of his "reconstruction experiment." In his official report, Schurz reported racial violence toward freedmen, but Johnson ignored Schurz's recommendations.

A photograph of Carl Schurz taken by Matthew Brady Studios

In 1867, Schurz moved to St. Louis, Missouri, and became the editor of the very powerful German-language newspaper, the *Westliche Post*. One of the men employed as a reporter during this time by Schurz was another German immigrant, Joseph Pulitzer. Pulitzer would go on to become a highly successful publisher.

As an editor, Schurz became concerned with corruption and reform. In 1868, he was elected to the U.S. Senate where he served from 1869 to 1875. He led most of the Illinois and Missouri German-Americans into the Liberal Republican Party of 1872, and he backed Horace Greeley for president against his old commander, Ulysses S. Grant. The election was a bitter one, but Grant was reelected in 1872.

The way back into national politics was not easy for Schurz. He had backed the wrong candidate in the 1872 election, and in politics, loyalty is considered a basic requirement. Nevertheless, Schurz used his political connections to push for the election of the reform-minded presidential candidate in 1876—Rutherford B. Hayes.

This time, Schurz's man won, and in 1877, Schurz became the Secretary of the Interior in the Hayes administration. In this position, he pushed for fair treatment of Native Americans and for reforming the civil service system—the hiring or appointing of government employees.

In 1881, Schurz left government service and moved to New York. He became the editor of the *New York Evening Post* in 1881. He wrote articles and gave speeches about the need to reform civil service. From 1892 to 1901, he served as president of the National Civil Service Reform League. He wrote editorials for *Harper's Weekly* from 1892 to 1898.

Schurz died on May 14, 1906, in New York. A reformer and statesman, Schurz boldly spoke out against slavery and corruption in government.

American Leaders & Innovators: Colonial Times to Reconstruction   Carl Schurz

Name: _____   Date: _____

Recalling Key Details

1. Why did Carl Schurz immigrate to the United States?

2. How was Schurz rewarded for his work on Lincoln's 1860 presidential campaign?

3. What was Schurz's greatest contribution to the Civil War?

4. Why did President Johnson send Schurz to visit Southern states?

5. What is the meaning of the word **freedmen** as it is used in paragraph three of the reading selection?

6. What were Schurz's achievements during the Hayes Administration?

7. What actions did Carl Schurz take to bring about reform to the Civil Service System?

American Leaders & Innovators: Colonial Times to Reconstruction   Carl Schurz

Name: _____ Date: _____

Activity

A **political cartoon** is a cartoon or comic strip created to communicate a social or political message. Thomas Nast, a famous cartoonist, used political cartoons to express his opinion.

Government agents, politicians, businessmen, adventurers, and others from the North who traveled to the South during the Reconstruction period were called **carpetbaggers**.

Directions: Examine the political cartoon. Use your observations and information from the reading selection to answer each question.

1. What is the central theme of the cartoon?

2. Who is the man caricaturized in the cartoon?

3. What are two ways Nast reveals the man's identity?

4. What message is Nast trying to convey?

Blanche Kelso Bruce 1841–1898

READING SELECTION

Blanche Kelso Bruce was born near Farmville, Prince Edward County, Virginia, on March 1, 1841. His mother was a slave and his father was a white plantation owner. Bruce's family moved to Missouri when Bruce was a boy. Bruce was tutored alongside his master's children.

Sometime after the start of the Civil War, Bruce escaped to Kansas and tried to enlist in the Union Army, but his enlistment application was rejected. He remained in Lawrence and became a teacher. In 1864, he returned to Hannibal, Missouri, and opened Missouri's first school for African-American children.

In 1868, after the South was reoccupied through the Military Reconstruction Act, Bruce moved to Mississippi, where he not only became the owner of a 640-acre cotton plantation but an owner of considerable property as well. He also taught for a while and sought political office. He would go on to serve as tax assessor, sheriff of Bolivar County, and a member of the Board of Levee Commissioners of Mississippi.

Blanche Bruce was the first African American to serve a full term in the U.S. Senate.

In 1874, he was elected to the United States Senate from Mississippi. While Bruce was not the first African American to serve in the U.S. Senate, he was the first to be elected to serve a full term. On his first day as a senator, Bruce gained a powerful ally in Republican Senator Conkling of New York. Conkling mentored Bruce on the rules and procedures of the Senate and helped to get him assigned to important committees such as Education and Labor, Manufactures, and Pensions.

Bruce served in the Senate for six years—to the actual end of Reconstruction—and as a legislator, he compiled an interesting record. He was involved in numerous debates over election fraud and civil rights in the South. He opposed the various policies designed to keep Chinese immigrants from American shores and took the side of Native Americans in various struggles with the federal government. He even worked to obtain a form of amnesty for ex-Confederates in Mississippi.

One of his major concerns seems to have been federal aid in harnessing the Mississippi River. He worked for flood control and the improvement of navigation facilities, and he argued that foreign commerce should be encouraged to enter various ports along the river.

When Reconstruction ended, so did Bruce's senatorial career. However, he stayed on in Washington, and President Garfield made him the Registrar of the Treasury, a position he held until 1885. In 1889, President Harrison appointed him Recorder of Deeds for the District of Columbia. This was not an insignificant position. Still later, after the election of President McKinley, Bruce was once again made the Registrar of the Treasury.

Blanche K. Bruce died in Washington, D.C., on March 17, 1898. He spent his life championing and protecting the rights of emancipated slaves and other minorities.

Recalling Key Details

1. How did Blanche Kelso Bruce receive his childhood education?

2. What contribution did Bruce make to the education of African-American children in Missouri?

3. What local or state political offices did Bruce hold in Mississippi?

4. What distinction does Bruce hold in the U.S. Senate?

5. How did Senator Conkling help Bruce become an effective senator?

6. What is the meaning of the word *emancipated* as it is used in paragraph eight of the reading selection?

7. What causes did Blanche Kelso Bruce champion as a U.S. senator?

American Leaders & Innovators: Colonial Times to Reconstruction   Blanche Kelso Bruce

Name: _____ Date: _____

Activity

As of 2017, only Blanche Kelso Bruce and nine other African Americans have served in the U.S. Senate: Hiram Revels, Edward Brooke, Carol Moseley Braun, Barack Obama, Roland W. Burris, Tim Scott, William "Mo" Cowan, Cory A. Booker, and Kamala Harris.

Directions: Select one of the nine U.S. senators listed above and research their senatorial careers. Complete the graphic organizer.

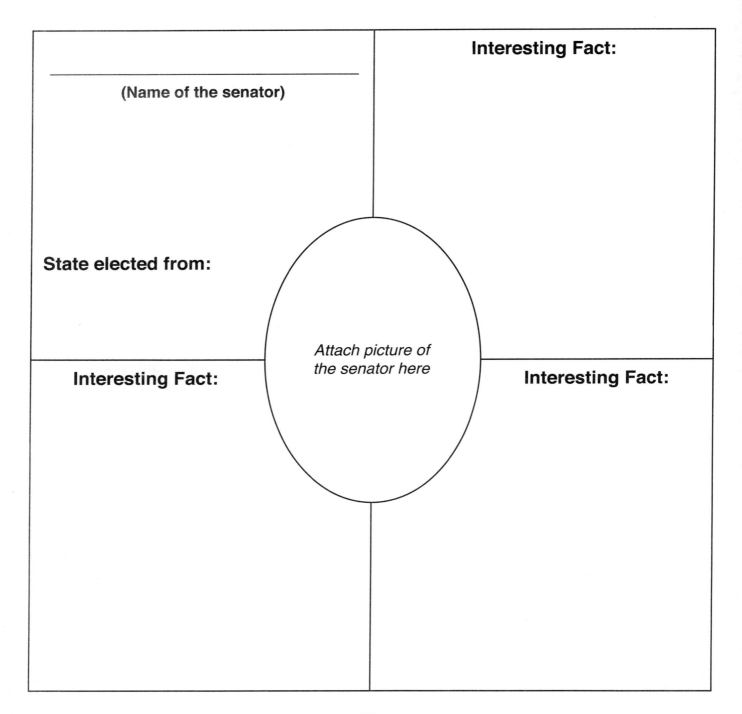

Answer Keys

Recalling Key Details: Roger Williams (p. 3)
1. no statues, rituals, or bishops in worship
2. religious views made him unpopular in England
3. separation of church and state
4. his views on religious freedom, and his proclaiming the king had no right to charter Native American tribal land to colonists
5. colony welcomed religious minorities such as Baptists, Quakers, and Jews
6. one who separates from the established religion
7. His views of separation of church and state and religious freedom probably inspired the writers of the U.S. Constitution and the Bill of Rights.

Recalling Key Details: Benjamin Franklin (p. 6)
1. He came up from poverty to wealth and political success through his own efforts.
2. to train under an expert for the purpose of learning a trade or business
3. *Pennsylvania Gazette*
4. included weather and agricultural predictions, charts of the moon's phases, and proverbs
5. improved mail service; established special messenger services between cities; started world's first subscription library; organized a fire department; reformed city police; started a program to pave and light streets; led the fight to establish a hospital
6. helped negotiate the Treaty of Paris
7. He helped write the Declaration of Independence, negotiate the Treaty of Paris, and signed the Constitution of the United States.

Activity: Benjamin Franklin (p. 7)
(Answers will vary, but may include)
1. It takes a lot of hard work to build a good reputation, but only one bad deed can destroy it quickly.
2. If you say or do something when you are angry, you will be ashamed of yourself later.
3. You should always tell the truth.
4. If one does things hastily, he will waste time correcting his mistakes.
5. It is easier to never start a habit than to stop it.

Recalling Key Details: James Otis (p. 9)
1. allowed customs officers to enter any premises or area during daylight in order to determine the possibility of illegal importation or smuggling
2. the Writs of Assistance were "instruments of slavery"
3. complaints
4. passing taxes onto the colonists without their ability to speak in opposition is oppression
5. required a revenue stamp be placed on legal documents, newspapers, and marriage licenses
6. imposed taxes upon imports into the colonies
7. He helped create a list of the colonists' grievances that was sent to the King. This led to the repeal of the Stamp Act.

Recalling Key Details: Benjamin Banneker (p. 12)
1. first wooden clock built in North America
2. lent Banneker books on science and astronomy and some astronomical instruments
3. weather forecasts, tide tables, poems, anti-slavery speeches and essays
4. distributed his almanacs and helped him gain influential societal connections
5. Secretary of the Academy of Sciences in Paris
6. to measure or set the boundaries of land
7. He was a member of the survey team that set the boundaries for the District of Columbia. He helped Major Ellicott redraw the plans from memory after L'Enfant resigned.

Activity: Benjamin Banneker (p. 13)
1. *Benjamin Banneker's Pennsylvania, Delaware, Maryland and Virginia Almanack and Ephemeris, for the Year of Our Lord, 1792*
2. 1980
3. tobacco
4. fire
5. locusts appear in large numbers every 17 years

Recalling Key Details: Francis Marion (p. 15)
1. because of his ability to escape his British pursuers in the swamps
2. On his first voyage the ship sank and he spent several days in a lifeboat without food and water.
3. He had to leave the battle, so he wasn't captured.
4. strategies involving surprise attacks and quick withdrawals
5. It was located on an island in the Pee Dee River.
6. Marion stole British supplies, drove off their horses, and freed American prisoners.
7. He developed a series of strategies known as guerrilla warfare, which helped him elude the British army while he raided their camps for supplies and freed captured soldiers.

Recalling Key Details: Thomas Paine (p. 18)
1. He failed at nearly everything he tried.
2. to encourage American colonists to rebel against the British government

American Leaders & Innovators: Colonial Times to Reconstruction   Answer Keys

3. to inspire soldiers and patriots to continue to fight after a series of losses to the British
4. one who loves, supports, and defends his country
5. to boost troop morale; to keep them in the army and fighting
6. He had attacked the character of George Washington.
7. His *Common Sense* and *The American Crisis* pamphlets promoted the idea of America's independence from Great Britain and inspired the colonists to continue fighting at a time when affairs were going badly for the Revolutionary cause.

Activity: Thomas Paine (p. 19)
(Answers will vary but may include)
1. America's desire for freedom is the desire of all mankind.
2. America's strength is not in the number of supporters but in their unity of purpose.
3. If colonists did not want to take part in the rebellion against Britain, they should not stand in the way of those who want independence.

Recalling Key Details: Joseph Warren (p. 21)
1. He graduated from Harvard University and did a kind of apprenticeship with a physician.
2. the enactment of the Stamp Act of 1765
3. anonymously wrote a series of newspaper articles in opposition to the acts
4. drafted protest letters stating the colonial arguments and sent them to Parliament and published them in the colonies
5. the formal determinations or positions of any association of individuals
6. a set of resolutions calling for the British to repeal the provisions of the Intolerable Acts
7. He wrote a series of articles in opposition to the Townshend Acts and served on the Committee of Correspondence that communicated their arguments to the British Parliament and the colonies. He drafted the Suffolk Resolves to protest the provisions of the Intolerable Acts.

Activity: Joseph Warren (p. 22)
April 18, 1775: As chairman of the Boston Committee of Safety, Warren dispatched Revere and Dawes to warn Samuel Adams and John Hancock that the British were coming to arrest them.
April 19, 1775: He left his medical practice and headed toward Lexington and Concord. He joined up with militiamen firing at British soldiers retreating back to Charlestown. He also provided medical care to wounded American militiamen.

May 10, 1775: He approved of Benedict Arnold's plan to capture the cannons at Fort Ticonderoga. Warren and the Committee of Safety supplied Arnold with gunpowder and bayonets.

Recalling Key Details: John Jay (p. 24)
1. ended war between America and Great Britain
2. John Jay, Benjamin Franklin, John Adams, and Henry Laurens
3. people who supported ratification of the Constitution
4. series of 85 essays promoting the Constitution
5. John Jay, Alexander Hamilton, and James Madison
6. declared the United States' neutrality in any conflicts between France and Great Britain
7. One of the authors of *The Federalist Papers*, he supported the ratification of the Constitution.

Recalling Key Details: Tecumseh (p. 27)
1. a Shawnee warrior and leader who tried to halt America's westward expansion
2. to prevent the expansion of the United States into the Northwest Territory
3. He was a gifted speaker with the ability to inspire others.
4. agreement between two or more parties
5. concern over the tribal alliances formed by Tecumseh
6. British guns were left behind at the Battle of Tippecanoe.
7. He dedicated his life to uniting tribes east of the Mississippi River to defend their lands against American westward expansion. He opposed treaties. He fought on the side of the British in the War of 1812.

Recalling Key Details: Dolley Madison (p. 30)
1. Guilford County, North Carolina
2. 1809
3. worked with architect to decorate and furnish the presidential mansion
4. known for her charm and social grace as a hostess
5. wife of the president of the United States
6. War of 1812
7. She saved a famous painting of President George Washington and a number of very valuable presidential papers during the British invasion of Washington during the War of 1812.

Recalling Key Details: Winfield Scott (p. 33)
1. War of 1812, Mexican War, Civil War
2. clearing banks of the Niagara River allowed Oliver Perry to get his small fleet into Lake Erie
3. helped with organizing and training the army
4. impressed with how he governed the capital city of Mexico with justice
5. already a politician; Democratic Party united
6. withdrawn from

7. He wrote the manual of arms for organizing and training the army. It was used through the Civil War. His invasion of Mexico during the Mexican War was one of the greatest campaigns of all time. His Anaconda Plan was used by Lincoln to defeat the South.

Activity: Winfield Scott (p. 34)
Objective: naval blockade of Southern ports
Objective: take control of Confederate strongholds on the Mississippi River in order to divide the Confederacy and cut off supply lines

Recalling Key Details: Benjamin Lundy (p. 36)
1. opponent of slavery
2. Quakers were active in the anti-slavery movement.
3. *The Genius of Universal Emancipation*
4. both wanted to recolonize former slaves
5. William Lloyd Garrison; both abolitionists
6. opposition to the annexation of Texas
7. He traveled the country publishing his anti-slavery newspaper *The Genius;* he organized anti-slavery societies.

Recalling Key Details: David Glasgow Farragut (p. 39)
1. Captain David Porter
2. War of 1812
3. Union
4. failure to order him to attack Mobile Bay
5. ships (vessels)
6. Battle of Mobile Bay
7. He captured Mobile Bay, the last Confederate-controlled seaport on the Gulf of Mexico, and he bombarded Vicksburg.

Recalling Key Details: Dorothea Lynde Dix (p. 42)
1. teacher
2. inspired her to seek reforms for prison conditions and treatment of the mentally ill
3. people who take action to improve something from bad to good
4. Insane people were being kept in cages, closets, cellars, stalls, and pens. They were chained, naked, beaten with rods, and lashed.
5. mentally ill persons no longer kept in prisons with criminals; states built asylums to treat mentally ill
6. recruited, trained and organized female nurses for the Union Army
7. She worked to bring about reforms for the treatment of the mentally ill, not only in North America but also in Europe. The mentally ill were no longer kept in prisons with criminals, but asylums were built for their treatment and care. Mentally ill patients were treated more humanely.

Activity: Dorothea Lynde Dix (p. 43)
Jane Addams: co-founded Hull House, a settlement in Chicago that provided community services to poor immigrants
Dorothea Lynde Dix: reformer for the treatment and care of the mentally ill
Frederick Douglass: African-American abolitionist, author, and speaker for the anti-slavery movement
William Lloyd Garrison: abolitionist crusader who published the anti-slavery newspaper *The Liberator*
Julia Ward Howe: advocated for women's suffrage and the abolitionist movement
Helen Hunt Jackson: advocated for the rights of Native Americans
Horace Mann: promoted public education
Lucretia Mott: abolitionist and women's rights activist
Sojourner Truth: African-American abolitionist and women's rights advocate
Frances Willard: advocated for the prohibition of alcohol and for women's right to vote

Recalling Key Details: Justin Smith Morrill (p. 45)
1. owned a store; wise business investments
2. Whig Party died
3. a representative
4. to increase taxes on goods imported into the United States
5. almost 32 years
6. Kansas
7. He led the passage of the Morrill Acts of 1862 and 1890. The 1862 act established land-grant colleges and universities in each of the fifty states for the teaching of agricultural and mechanic arts. The 1890 act provided additional funding for 1862 land-grant institutions and led to the establishment of African-American land-grant colleges and universities.

Activity: Justin Smith Morrill (p. 46)
Hatch Act of 1887: provided funding for the creation of agricultural experiment stations connected to land-grant colleges and universities
Second Morrill Act of 1890: provided additional funding for 1862 land-grant institutions and led to the establishment of African-American land-grant colleges and universities
Smith-Lever Act of 1914: established Cooperative Extension Services associated with each land-grant institution
Land-Grant Status Act of 1994: granted land-grant status to Native-American tribal colleges and universities

Recalling Key Details: Harriet Beecher Stowe (p. 48)
1. violations or wrongs
2. as a social sin, not an individual sin
3. opposed it
4. her sister-in-law

5. During a Sunday church service, she had visions of a slave granting forgiveness to the person abusing him. She also thought about the stories she was told by escaped slaves.
6. bestseller; sold 300,000 copies in the first year in the U.S. and 1.5 million in England; translated into over 60 languages.
7. It brought the issue of slavery out into the open as never before. Through the characters of the book, people began to see slaves as real people suffering terrible injustices.

Activity: Harriet Beecher Stowe (p. 49)
1. freedom, maternal love, or Christian faith
2. She risked death for her and her son in the frozen river to gain their freedom.
3. God will bless those who help the "sore distressed."

Recalling Key Details: Elizabeth Cady Stanton (p. 51)
1. tutored her in Greek, Latin, and mathematics, subjects girls didn't usually study
2. lawyer
3. insisted on the adoption of a resolution calling for women's suffrage
4. lecturing, writing, and organizing local feminist groups
5. the right of all people to vote regardless of sex, race, social status, or wealth
6. Elizabeth: more skillful speaker; Susan: more patient and better at organizing
7. She helped organize the first women's rights convention. She spent time on the cause of women's rights—lecturing, writing, and organizing local feminist groups. She helped organize the National American Woman Suffrage Association and was its first president. In 1868, she helped establish *Revolution,* a magazine devoted to women's rights. She co-produced three enormous volumes of the *History of Woman Suffrage.*

Recalling Key Details: Carl Schurz (p. 54)
1. involved in the failed 1848 German revolutions
2. appointed as U.S. Minister to Spain
3. kept German-Americans supporting the Union
4. to investigate conditions in Southern states and to see how reconstruction was working
5. freed slaves
6. pushed for fair treatment of Native Americans and for reforming the civil service system
7. He wrote newspaper articles and editorials and gave speeches about the need to reform the civil service system and end corruption in government. He served as president of the National Civil Service Reform League.

Activity: Carl Schurz (p. 55)
1. Carpetbaggers
2. Carl Schurz
3. face is a likeness of Carl Schurz; name on the money bag carried on his back; also says "from Wisconsin to Missouri"
4. Carl Schurz is a carpetbagger.

Recalling Key Details: Blanche Kelso Bruce (p. 57)
1. tutored alongside his master's children
2. opened Missouri's first school for African-American children
3. tax assessor, sheriff, member of the Board of Levee Commissioners of Mississippi
4. first African American to be elected to serve a full term in the U.S. Senate
5. mentored him on Senate rules and procedures; helped get him appointed to important committees
6. freed
7. During his six years in the Senate, he spoke out about election fraud and civil rights abuses in the South. He opposed policies designed to keep Chinese immigrants from American shores. He took the side of Native Americans in various struggles with the federal government. He worked for flood control and the improvement of navigation facilities on the Mississippi River. He argued that foreign commerce should be encouraged to enter various ports along the river.